Primary Sources of American Treaties™

The Treaty of Paris, 1783

A Primary Source Examination of the Treaty That Recognized American Independence

Lee Jedson

rosen central
Primary Source™
The Rosen Publishing Group, Inc., New York

To One Eye and Jigs

Published in 2006 by The Rosen Publishing Group, Inc.
29 East 21st Street, New York, NY 10010

First Edition

Library of Congress Cataloging-in-Publication Data

Jedson, Lee.
The Treaty of Paris, 1783: a primary source examination of the treaty that recognized
American Independence/Lee Jedson.—1st ed.
     p. cm.—(Primary sources of American treaties)
Includes bibliographical references and index.
ISBN 1-4042-0441-5 (lib. bdg.)
1. United States—History—Revolution, 1775–1783—Peace—Juvenile literature.
2. Great Britain. Treaties, etc. United States, 1783 Sept. 3—Juvenile literature.
3. United States—History—Revolution, 1775–1783—Juvenile literature. 4. United
States—History—Colonial period, ca. 1600–1775—Juvenile literature. I. Title.
II. Series.
E249.J443 2006
973.3'17—dc22

2004027818

Manufactured in the United States of America

On the cover: A 1783 painting entitled *The Signing of the Treaty of Paris* by Benjamin West, which shows the following from left to right: John Jay, John Adams, Benjamin Franklin, Henry Laurens, and Franklin's grandson William Temple Franklin.

Contents

and in Virtue of our full Power
with our Hands the present De
Treaty, and caused the Seals of our

Introduction

The year was 1782. After close to seven years of bitter war with its American colonies, Great Britain had decided to surrender. At the time, Britain had the most feared and respected military force in the world. In the end, however, its soldiers had proved no match for the brave and determined American troops that had been fighting courageously for American independence.

In April, the British government voted to end the war with America. During the summer, British troops were ordered to begin leaving Britain's former colonies. On November 30, 1782, a trial peace agreement was signed in Paris, France. Two months later, on February 4, 1783, Great Britain formally announced that it would permanently stop all fighting. However, a definitive treaty was required to guarantee peace between the United States and Great Britain.

To negotiate the terms of this treaty with the British, the new American government counted on three of its most talented diplomats: John Jay, John Adams, and Benjamin Franklin. The one item the three Americans insisted upon in

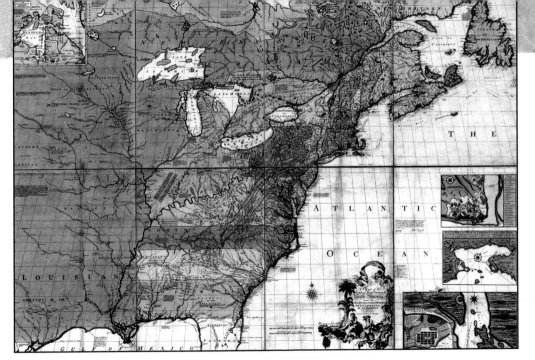

Above is a hand-colored map showing the British and French territories in North America. The map indicates the location of roads, borders, settlement boundaries, and distances between one place and another. The insets include Labrador and Hudson Bay, a plan of Halifax in Nova Scotia, and a plan of the old city of Quebec.

---

the treaty was Britain's recognition of the independence of the United States of America. Originally, the French were to have acted as negotiators between Jay, Adams, Franklin, and British representatives. However, because French diplomats were distracted by conflicts with Spain, American and British representatives met secretly among themselves. With intelligence and goodwill, they produced a treaty whose ten articles were agreed upon by both parties.

Signed on September 3, 1783, and ratified the following year, the Treaty of Paris became the first official document to fully recognize the independence of the new American nation. As such, along with the Declaration of Independence and the U.S. Constitution, it ranks as one of the major documents responsible for the creation of the United States of America.

1

Thirteen Colonies

In the early 1600s, England began establishing colonies along the Atlantic coast of North America—from Newfoundland in the north to Florida in the south. The first successful colony was Virginia. It was here that, in 1607, the settlement of Jamestown was founded. Over the next century, many immigrants traveled across the Atlantic Ocean. Most came from England, but some came from other western European nations. Many of these adventurers were in search of new opportunities and a place where they could practice their religions without being persecuted. They also wanted freedom from the centuries' old rules and traditions of a continent governed by kings and queens. In the Old World, there was little tolerance for different religions and little chance of improving one's economic fortunes.

⇒ The Founding of the Thirteen Colonies ⇐

Between 1607 and 1733, thirteen colonies were founded along the East Coast of North America. After Virginia came Massachusetts (1620), New Hampshire (1623), Maryland (1634), Connecticut (circa 1635), Rhode Island (1636),

Delaware (1638), North Carolina (1653), South Carolina (1663), New York (1664), New Jersey (1664), Pennsylvania (1682), and Georgia (1732).

Throughout the 1600s and 1700s, news of the opportunities available in the American colonies reached England. Stories of endless land and tolerant local governments were very appealing to those who had suffered under the British monarchy. The problem was that aristocratic families owned much of the land, and "commoners," as the non-aristocrats were known, had very few rights. In 1700, the population of the colonies was 250,000. By 1775, this number had grown to almost 2.5 million. At the time, this was nearly one-third of Britain's population.

Eventually, the separate colonies forged ties with one another. Roads allowed increased travel and trade. Meanwhile, newspapers kept residents of one colony informed about what was happening in the others. Over time, colonists adapted to the different realities of the New World. They began to create their own lifestyles and culture. Gradually, residents of the thirteen colonies discovered they had much in common with one other. They also felt less connected to the Old World they had left across the Atlantic Ocean.

⚘ No Government Representation ⚘

From the beginning, England had no specific idea of how its thirteen colonies in North America would be administered. Some colonies had their own independent governments. Meanwhile, others were governed by representatives of the king. As subjects of the British crown, citizens of all the

KING GEORGE III

Between 1760 and 1820, George III was the king of England. Following the death of his grandfather, George II, George was crowned when he was a young man. In need of a suitable wife, Princess Sophia Charlotte, daughter of a German duke, was chosen to be George III's queen. The couple went on to have a happy marriage. Together they raised fifteen children—more than any other English monarch.

Under George III's long reign, Britain experienced the birth of industry, many bitter wars with France, and

This political cartoon from 1782 depicts America, symbolized by a Native American woman (right), *celebrating the territory she has acquired. Her French allies* (middle three) *are angry because they have lost a lot, including limbs that lie symbolically at the feet of King George III* (left), *and have not received anything for their help.*

the expansion and subsequent loss of most of its North American colonies. Although some colonists were loyal to the king, many eventually grew to hate George III. They thought of him as a symbol of repression and tyranny. Shortly after the colonies achieved independence, George III began to suffer from severe mental illness. Ultimately, this made him incapable of governing.

American colonies had to obey the laws created by the king and the British parliament. The problem was that many laws passed by the British government were in the best interest of the English living in England and not of those in the colonies.

In 1764, England passed the Currency Act. The new law specified that only Britain could make money and control the amount of currency that was in circulation. The colonies also suffered under the Navigation Acts. These were a series of laws that limited the colonists from competing with British businesses. Restrictions prevented merchants from selling products to countries other than Britain— specifically France and Spain. Even if other countries were willing to pay higher prices for goods, the colonies could only trade with Britain. Also, they were only allowed to trade at prices that were set by British merchants.

Some colonists thought this was very unfair. At the very least, they felt that they deserved to have government representation in the British parliament in order to vote on laws. However, in its defense, the British government said that its own officials in the colonies represented American interests. Frustrated, the colonies began to ignore some of the British laws. In fact, they created their own laws. This situation led to rising tension between Britain and the thirteen colonies.

⚊ The French and Indian War ⚊

In the 1750s, France and England were at war in Europe. France also had large colonies in North America. These consisted of Louisiana (a vast area extending throughout the Mississippi Valley and the Gulf Coast) and New France (later part of Canada). With both countries seeking control of more of the continent's natural riches, it was only a matter of time before the war spread to North America.

In 1754, the French attacked England's thirteen American colonies. The French and Indian War saw British troops and American colonists fighting against French troops and their Native American allies. England eventually won the war in 1759, with the capture of Quebec. In 1763, the Treaty of Paris was signed, officially ending the war. Under its conditions, France lost all of its North American territories, with the exception of the tiny islands of Saint-Pierre and Miquelon, off the Canadian coast.

Although Britain had won the war, nine years of fighting had been costly. Meanwhile, Britain feared further attacks from other European nations hoping for North American territories of their own. To defend its interests, England sent

The lush scene in this engraving (a copy of the original painting) by Benjamin West illustrates the death of British general James Wolfe during the French and Indian War. Surrounded by Native Americans and a soldier, Wolfe is slowly dying from a fatal wound received in battle. His death came at the same moment when his troops won the war against the French in New France, which is now known as Quebec. A courageous war hero, he is also famous for his last words, "God be praised I will Die in peace."

troops to the thirteen colonies. However, the king had no money left to pay them. In an attempt to generate new funds, George III decided to tax the colonists.

In 1764, Britain passed the Sugar Act, which placed a tax on all the sugar the colonies purchased from the French and Spanish. In 1765, it passed the Stamp Act. This law required all colonial newspapers and legal documents to carry a stamp purchased from the British government. In effect, this was a tax. Other taxes were put on goods such as fabrics and coffee. Enraged at these unjust taxes, many colonists

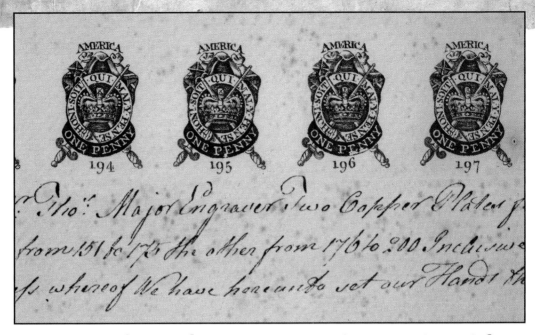

This is a proof sheet of one-penny stamps that was submitted for approval to the Commissioners of Stamps by an engraver on May 10, 1765. According to the Stamp Act, one-penny stamps were to be used on newspapers, pamphlets, and all other papers that were larger than half a sheet but not more than a whole sheet.

---

organized protests. In Boston, a group of angry workers and tradesmen formed a secret protest group called the Sons of Liberty. Soon, there were Sons of Liberty groups in all of the colonies. In the meantime, leaders of all the colonies met to express their outrage with the Stamp Act. Things simply could not continue as they were.

2

Talking About a Revolution

emonstrations by angry colonists forced the British government to do away with the Stamp Act and reduce taxes on sugar. However, in 1767, the British government passed new taxes on goods such as glass, paper, paint, and tea. These products were all shipped from Britain to the colonies. The taxes on them were known as the Townshend Acts, named after Britain's prime minister at the time, Charles Townshend.

Furious, the colonists refused to purchase any British goods. They argued that since they weren't represented in Parliament, they shouldn't have to pay any taxes. Their famous phrase of protest was "No taxation without representation," meaning that the British government had no right to tax citizens who had no say in how they were being governed. The colonists' anger caused the British government to repeal the Townshend Acts in 1770.

Nonetheless, tensions between colonists and Britain continued to grow. Many wealthy landowners and business-men were tired of the British regulating their activities. Colonists with less money resented paying such high taxes

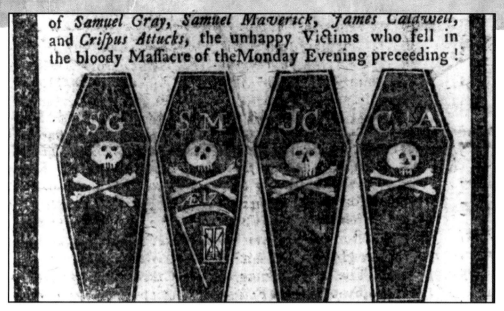

This newspaper column shows four coffins featuring the first and last initials of four men who were killed during the Boston Massacre: Samuel Gray, Samuel Maverick, James Caldwell, and Crispus Attucks. The text shown above lists the names of the men and identifies them as "the unhappy Victims who fell in the bloody Ma[ss]acre of the Monday Evening preceeding!"

for imported goods. Throughout the colonies, people were becoming increasingly fed up.

⇒ The Boston Massacre ⇐

The colonists' anger was increased by the presence of British soldiers patrolling their towns. The red-coated soldiers were yet another reminder of British authority. In Boston, citizens began to verbally and physically attack British soldiers. Tension grew and finally erupted on the night of March 5, 1770. On this evening, some angry citizens began taunting a British soldier guarding the Customs House. They yelled insults and threw snowballs at him. A crowd eventually formed and other soldiers soon arrived. In the commotion, someone yelled "Fire!" and the soldiers began shooting into the crowd. Five townspeople were killed. Another five were wounded.

Although the soldiers were put on trial, they were all set free. This episode became known as the Boston Massacre. The five citizens who were killed were the first to have died for the cause of American independence.

The Boston Tea Party

In 1773, the British passed the Tea Act. This law allowed the British East India Company (a group that had controlled all tea trade between Britain and its colonies) to sell tea to Americans at lower prices than those offered by other countries. The British parliament did this knowing that the colonists would be unable to refuse buying English tea that was so inexpensive. In doing so, however, colonists would end up paying the taxes placed on the tea. Prior to this act, the colonists had been buying tea illegally from Dutch companies. They did this to avoid paying taxes to Britain.

The colonists were furious and demanded that the government repeal the Tea Act. In the port of Boston, dockworkers refused to unload the tea from ships. The governor of Massachusetts insisted upon the unloading of the tea and payment of the taxes. Instead, on the evening of December 16, 1773, about sixty members of the Sons of Liberty went to Boston Harbor. Disguised as Mohawk Indians, they boarded the ships and dumped forty-five tons of tea into the harbor.

An Eyewitness Account

The following is an excerpt from an eyewitness account of George Hewes, a member of the Sons of Liberty who participated in what became known as the Boston Tea Party:

This is a drawing of George Robert Twelves Hewes, one of the members of the Boston Tea Party. Hewes, a poor shoemaker from Boston, joined the resistance movement in 1768. While the British soldiers were trying to bring order to the streets during the riots, Hewes was caught in the middle of cross fire, but survived.

It was now evening, and I immediately dressed myself in the costume of an Indian, equipped with a small hatchet, which I and my associates denominated the tomahawk, with which, and a club, after having painted my face and hands with coal dust in the shop of a blacksmith, I repaired to Griffin's wharf, where the ships lay that contained the tea. When I first appeared in the street after being thus disguised, I fell in with many who were dressed, equipped and painted as I was, and who fell in with me and marched in order to the place of our destination.

When we arrived at the wharf, there were three of our number who assumed an authority to direct our operations, to which we readily submitted. They divided us into three parties, for the purpose of boarding. The three ships contained the tea at the same time. The name of him who commanded the division to which I was assigned was Leonard Pitt. The names of the other commanders I never knew . . .

We were immediately ordered . . . to board all the ships at the same time . . . The commander of the division to which I belonged, as soon as we were on board the ship appointed me boatswain, and ordered me to go to the captain and demand of him the keys to the hatches and a dozen candles. I made the demand accordingly, and the captain promptly replied, and delivered the articles; but requested me at the same time to do no damage to the ship or rigging.

We then were ordered by our commander to open the hatches and take out all the chests of tea and throw them overboard, and we immediately proceeded to execute his orders, first cutting and splitting the chests with our tomahawks, so as thoroughly to expose them to the effects of the water.

In about three hours from the time we went on board, we had thus broken and thrown overboard every tea chest to be found in the ship, while those in the other ships were disposing of the tea in the same way, at the same time. We were surrounded by British armed ships, but no attempt was made to resist us.

We then quietly retired to our several places of residence, without having any conversation with each other, or taking any measures to discover who were our associates; nor do I recollect of our having had the knowledge of the name of a single individual concerned in that affair, except that of Leonard Pitt, the commander of my division . . . There appeared to

Americans throwing the Cargoes of the Tea Ships into the River, at Boston

Boston Tea Party, *W. D. Cooper's 1789 engraving, depicts a group of men from Boston who were disguised as Mohawk Indians. They are dumping some of the 342 wooden chests filled with Darjeeling tea (from India) into the waters below. The colonists wore disguises in order to board the tea ships that were at dock at the Boston Harbor.*

be an understanding that each individual should volunteer his services, keep his own secret, and risk the consequence for himself. No disorder took place during that transaction, and it was observed at that time that the stillest night ensued that Boston had enjoyed for many months.

Angered by this revolt, the British parliament closed Boston Harbor until the people of Boston had paid for the destroyed tea as well as the taxes on the tea. It also banned Massachusetts's elected government council, replacing its members with representatives chosen by the king. Public meetings were also banned and citizens were forced to house

British soldiers in their homes. The outraged citizens of Massachusetts and other colonies referred to these laws as the Intolerable Acts.

The British hoped that the Intolerable Acts would teach the people of Massachusetts a lesson and show the other colonies what would happen if they disobeyed English rule. Instead, it sparked the desire for independence from Britain. Outraged citizens from all of the colonies joined together against Britain. Leaders from each of the colonies called for a meeting to discuss what action they would take. This meeting was known as the First Continental Congress. Each colony elected members to attend the congress and represent its citizens. Leaders from all the colonies except for Georgia met in Philadelphia in 1774. Although they didn't yet seek independence from Britain, they decided to stick together and demand that Britain accept their list of colonial rights. They also promised to boycott the purchase of British products until Britain gave in to their demands.

Instead of negotiating with the colonial leaders, King George III decided to punish the colonies. In fact, he seemed to be encouraging conflict. As he wrote at the time: "The lines have been drawn. Blows must decide." While refusing to suspend the Intolerable Acts, he sent British forces to block access to valuable fishing territories in the North Atlantic. This decision resulted in violence. The colonies' armed volunteers (known as militiamen) grouped together and tried to drive British soldiers out of Boston. At the same time, battles broke out at Lexington and Concord. These were the first battles of the American Revolution.

⌐ The Second Continental Congress ⌐

Because the king of England had refused to recognize the colonies' rights, the thirteen American colonies decided to take action. On May 10, 1775 (three weeks after the first shots of the Revolution were fired), delegates from each of the colonies met in Philadelphia for the Second Continental Congress. The congress's delegates decided that together they would form a new government that was prepared to resist British rule. The congress was held in the Pennsylvania State House, which is now called Independence Hall. Among the delegates were John Hancock from Massachusetts, Thomas Jefferson from Virginia, and Benjamin Franklin from Pennsylvania. Members of the congress were prepared to go to war against Britain. They decided that the colonies' individual groups of militiamen would fight together as one larger unit called the Continental army. George Washington was elected as the new army's commander in chief.

Washington, a wealthy Virginia plantation owner, had earned a reputation as a brave, loyal, and resourceful general during the French and Indian War (1754–1763). In 1758, he had become a member of the House of Burgesses. This was an elected group of landowners that governed Virginia. After Britain outlawed the House of Burgesses in 1774, Washington was chosen as one of the delegates to represent Virginia in both Continental Congresses. On July 3, 1775, Washington took charge of the first American army. The soldiers were poorly trained and had very little equipment, but they were determined to fight for their rights.

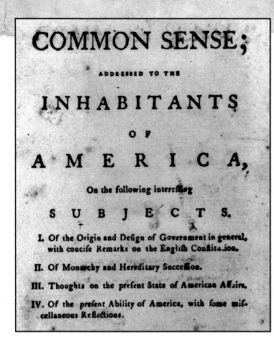

COMMON SENSE;

ADDRESSED TO THE

INHABITANTS

OF

AMERICA,

On the following interesting

SUBJECTS.

I. Of the Origin and Design of Government in general,
with concise Remarks on the English Constitution.

II. Of Monarchy and Hereditary Succession.

III. Thoughts on the present State of American Affairs.

IV. Of the present Ability of America, with some miscellaneous Reflections.

This is the title page of Thomas Paine's first edition of Common Sense, *printed in Philadelphia in 1776. Paine was communicating his belief that the colonists had the right to revolt against the unfair government that was ruling them. Ultimately, Paine's treatise would have an enormous impact on the future of the colonies.*

On January 10, 1776, Thomas Paine, an English writer and revolutionary living in Philadelphia, published a small book called *Common Sense*. In it, he described his idea of a government ruled by representatives elected by the people. Paine was the first person who openly demanded independence from England. Written in simple English, *Common Sense* was read by many colonial leaders, including George Washington, Thomas Jefferson, and hundreds of thousands of Americans. In the book, a hopeful Paine wrote: "We have it in our power to begin the world anew."

Common Sense was very much on the minds of the Continental Congress's members when they met in Virginia in May 1776. Delegates were no longer content to fight for their rights. Instead, many wanted total independence from Britain. The congress passed a resolution for the colonies to become free and independent states. They also chose a committee to write a formal declaration of independence. Assisted by Benjamin Franklin and John Adams, Thomas Jefferson was selected to write the first draft of the Declaration of Independence.

John Hancock ordered printer John Dunlap to print broadside copies of the Declaration of Independence. On July 8, 1776, between 200 and 500 copies were printed. The more familiar declaration was not completed until August 2, 1776, when the delegates added their signatures. Only twenty-five copies remain. See page 55 for a partial transcription.

⚞ The Declaration of Independence ⚟

The Declaration of Independence laid the foundations for a modern democratic government, which was a very new concept at the time. It stated that a government must be elected by the people in order to serve the people. In the introduction, the declaration states that "all men are created equal" and have the right to "life, liberty, and the pursuit of happiness." These words have come to sum up the ideals of American democracy and are treasured by many Americans today.

This important document also declared the thirteen colonies' independence and defended the rights of its citizens against British injustices. On July 2, 1776, the members of the Continental Congress voted in favor of independence from Britain. Two days later, on July 4, they all gathered to approve the Declaration of Independence. Subsequently, July 4 became known as American Independence Day. True freedom, however, would only come when the American colonists had fought and won it from the British.

3

War of Independence

The first gunshots that set off the American Revolution were fired in Lexington, Massachusetts. On April 19, 1775, British general Thomas Gage sent 700 soldiers to destroy guns and ammunition that the colonists had stored in Concord, a small town outside of Boston. Gage also had orders to arrest two revolutionary leaders: Samuel Adams and John Hancock.

Luckily, Americans discovered these plans beforehand. A metalsmith and revolutionary named Paul Revere was sent to warn colonists that Gage's troops were being shipped across Boston Harbor to begin their march on Lexington on the evening of April 18. That same evening, Revere hung two lanterns in the Old North Church steeple as a signal to the Americans that the British were coming. He then rode off on horseback to warn Adams and Hancock. By the time British troops had arrived in Lexington, both leaders had escaped.

In Lexington, the local militia was waiting for the British troops. They had organized themselves into a group called the minutemen. Their name came from the fact that they expected to go to battle at a minute's notice. Compared to

MIDNIGHT RIDER

Paul Revere's historic role in the Revolution was not very well known during his lifetime. However, in 1860, more than forty years after his death, it became the subject of a famous poem by the important American poet Henry Wadsworth Longfellow. Entitled "The Landlord's Tale; Paul Revere's Ride," it was part of a collection of poems called *Tales of a Wayside Inn*. One of the best-known poems in American history, it was often recited by future generations of American schoolchildren. Its famous opening lines are:

Listen, my children, and you shall hear
Of the midnight ride of Paul Revere,
On the eighteenth of April, in Seventy-five;
Hardly a man is now alive
Who remembers that famous day and year.

This is Grant Wood's 1931 oil painting The Midnight Ride of Paul Revere. *Wood was famous for depicting scenes of American life.*

hundreds of English soldiers, there were only seventy-five minutemen. When the British opened fire, eight minutemen were killed and ten were injured.

Thanks to Paul Revere and other messengers, by the time the British arrived in Concord, most of the arms and ammunitions had been taken to safe hiding places. British troops only succeeded in destroying some of the colonists' equipment. This British arrival set off fighting in Concord and the surrounding countryside. Colonists and British soldiers were killed and wounded. Fighting continued throughout the colonies, but tensions were particularly high in Boston, where British troops had occupied the city much to the anger of local citizens.

Shortly after the Declaration of Independence was signed, the British began launching attacks on the colonists. These were the first battles of what would become known as the Revolutionary War. The first battles waged between British and colonial soldiers were disastrous for the newly formed American army. Britain had many advantages over the new nation. First of all, Britain had much more money and a larger population. It also had the most powerful army and navy in the world, and both were very well trained and equipped. In contrast, American soldiers were a poorly trained, underfed collection of volunteers and local militia-men. They had fewer sophisticated arms and much less equipment. Their only advantage was that they were fighting on their own territory. Years of battles against Native Americans had given them a lot of experience in fighting in the wilderness.

This is a nineteenth-century copy of an original watercolor dating from 1777. In the painting, a typical American soldier of the time is shown carrying his bayonet. The original painting was made by German artist Captain Friedrich Konstantin von Germann, who served in the British army during the American Revolution.

An American Soldier.
1778

Washington's army finally met its first victory in Boston. The British had been holed up in Boston, surrounded by American troops. Then, on the evening of March 4, 1776, reinforcements arrived with more soldiers and fifty cannons. The next morning, when the British commander general William Howe awoke and saw so many cannons aimed at his ships, he rounded up his men and supplies and withdrew. They first went to Canada and then to New York City. In the fall of 1776, Washington and his Continental army marched to New York to greet them.

These initial battles were hard on Washington's 6,000 soldiers. By the year's end, those who hadn't been killed or injured were exhausted and hungry. In New York, the Continental army had suffered a string of defeats. After losing control of strategic forts, the British army had swept Washington and his troops off Long Island and Manhattan.

Christmas of 1776 found the dejected troops camped near Trenton, New Jersey, on the shores of the Delaware

River. To inspire them, Washington ordered his officers to read the troops "The Crisis," a new essay by Thomas Paine, which opened with these comforting words: "These are the times that try men's souls . . ."

Paine's words alone were not enough to encourage the soldiers. Washington desperately needed a victory to hold his troops together and to keep the hopes of the Revolution alive. Washington was willing to take a big risk to achieve this victory. Accordingly, on the evening of December 25, 1776, Washington led 2,500 soldiers across the Delaware River. A fierce snowstorm was raging and the ice-coated river was dangerous. Nonetheless, Washington's men snuck up on a nearby British camp in a surprise attack. They succeeded in killing more than 100 men and taking another thousand prisoners without one American being killed. The Battle of Trenton gave a big boost to the revolutionaries' cause. However, it wasn't until September 1777 that an American victory began to seem possible.

⌒ A Turning Point ⌒

For most of 1777, things had not looked promising for the Americans. In the fall, British troops began a campaign designed to cut off New England from the other colonies. In doing so, they hoped to divide the forces of already weakened and exhausted American soldiers. British general John Burgoyne led troops into upper New York from Canada while General Howe headed north from New York City. A British victory seemed likely. However, Burgoyne's troops found themselves slowed by the dense, overgrown forests of

AN AMERICAN MYTH

The dramatic Battle of Trenton became an American legend. It symbolized Washington's military genius and the bravery of the American revolutionaries. A renowned American senator named Henry Cabot Lodge was very moved by this story. In fact, he included the tale in a book he cowrote with his great friend, the adventurer and twenty-sixth American president of the United States, Theodore "Teddy" Roosevelt. Published in 1895, *Hero Tales from American History* helped immortalize the Battle of Trenton for future generations. As the authors point out in their introduction:

It is a good thing for all Americans, and it is an especially good thing for young Americans, to remember the men who have given their lives in war and peace to the service of their fellow-countrymen, and to keep in mind the feats of daring and personal prowess done in time past by some of the many champions of the nation in the various crises of her history.

On Christmas Eve[ning], when all the Christian world was feasting and rejoicing, and while the British were enjoying themselves in their comfortable quarters, Washington set out. With twenty four hundred men he crossed the Delaware through the floating ice, his boats managed and rowed by the sturdy fishermen of Marblehead from [Colonel John] Glover's regiment. The crossing was successful, and he landed about nine miles [14.5 kilometers] from

Trenton. It was bitter cold, and the sleet and snow drove sharply in the faces of the troops. [John] Sullivan, marching by the river, sent word that the arms of his soldiers were wet. "Tell your general," was Washington's reply to the message, "to use the bayonet, for the town must be taken." When they reached Trenton it was broad daylight. Washington, at the front and on the right of the line, swept down the Pennington road, and, as he drove back the

continued on page 30

This painting of Washington crossing the Delaware River depicts the famous moment when the general led his troops in a surprise attack against the British. Pictured here is a copy of the original painting by Emanuel Leutze. Although the actual crossing took place during a snowstorm at night, Leutze preferred the expressive and moody colors of a shimmering daytime sky.

continued from page 29

Hessian pickets, he heard the shout of Sullivan's men as, with Stark leading the van, they charged in from the river. A company of jaegers and of light dragoons slipped away. There was some fighting in the streets, but the attack was so strong and well calculated that resistance was useless. Colonel [Johann] Rahl, the British commander, aroused from his revels, was killed as he rushed out to rally his men, and in a few moments all was over. A thousand prisoners fell into Washington's hands, and this important detachment of the enemy was cut off and destroyed.

New York. Their progress was slow because their heavy cargo included thirty carts of Burgoyne's personal possessions and several very fragile cases of champagne (such habits had earned Burgoyne the nickname Gentleman Johnny in the American press).

By the time Burgoyne arrived near Saratoga, New York, American soldiers and local militiamen were laughing at his demands that they surrender. Led by General Horatio Gates, the American revolutionaries attacked Burgoyne's troops in what came to be known as the Battle of Saratoga. Cut off from Howe's forces (who were busy battling Washington's troops in the south), Burgoyne's troops were outnumbered by American soldiers by two to one. On October 17, 1777, the 7,700 British soldiers surrendered to the Americans. "The fortunes of war have made me your prisoner,"

Burgoyne declared as he handed over his sword to General Gates. "I shall always be ready to testify that it was through no fault of your excellency," replied Gates, graciously.

News of the astonishing British defeat spread rapidly through the colonies, filling the American patriots with hope. For months, American leaders had been asking French king Louis XVI for military and financial aid to help win the war. France, however, was cautious about helping a losing cause. Nonetheless, with victory suddenly possible, the colonists felt certain that Louis XVI would change his mind.

⌐ Winter at Valley Forge ⌐

In the winter of 1777 to 1778, George Washington and his army set up camp at Valley Forge, Pennsylvania, 25 miles (40 km) northeast of Philadelphia. It was a terribly cold winter with a great deal of snowfall. With only thin tents to protect them, the troops struggled just to survive. Many were without warm winter clothes or shoes. Over the winter, many soldiers died from cold, sickness, and hunger.

Fortunately, by February 1778, the situation had improved. The soldiers had built cabins equipped with fire-places for cooking and warmth. While waiting for spring to come and the fighting to start again, the troops trained hard. Washington received valuable help from Baron Friedrich Wilhelm von Steuben, a military officer from Prussia (present-day Germany) who had designed a training manual for the soldiers. By the time the winter was over, the Continental army was more organized, skillful, and stronger.

⚍ The French Join the War ⚎

After the Battle of Saratoga, the Continental Congress once again decided to seek French aid. Benjamin Franklin, the American minister to France, was sent to Paris to speak to Louis XVI and the French foreign minister. Still bitter from having lost the French and Indian War to England, France was eager to strike out against its old enemy. In February 1778, France and America signed a treaty that resulted in France entering into war with Britain. This treaty was the first official document that recognized America as a nation. The French immediately sent fleets of soldiers and supplies to America, the first of which arrived off the coast of Rhode Island in August.

One year later, Spain, an ally of France, also joined the Revolutionary War on the American side. This made things very difficult for Britain. Not only did the country face increased attacks in America, but it also had to defend its own territory from possible French and Spanish attacks in Europe.

⚍ Britain Surrenders ⚎

In spite of aid from France and Spain, between 1778 and 1780, the British continued to win major battles as they moved into the southern colonies. Britain's General Charles Cornwallis had reached South Carolina when General Nathanael Greene took charge of the American troops in the south. Greene decided that the only way to beat the British was to change tactics. Instead of fighting out in the open, Greene's men engaged in guerrilla warfare. Soldiers would hide in the bush, make surprise attacks on the enemy, and

This 1787 painting by John Trumbull, entitled The Surrender of Cornwallis at Yorktown, *shows French and American soldiers during the moments before an official truce was declared. Trumbull is renowned for being the first American painter to create a series of paintings that were thematically based on historical events.*

quickly retreat before the enemy had a chance to fight back. Using this strategy, the Americans drove the British to the coast and further north.

By the summer of 1781, American troops had forced Cornwallis and his men to Yorktown, Virginia. Yorktown was a port town from which Virginia's important tobacco crops were loaded and shipped off across the Atlantic. While American soldiers surrounded Yorktown, the French navy quickly entered nearby Chesapeake Bay. Cutting off the British fleet from possible aid, the French began attacking British ships that were stationed in the bay. After defeating the British navy, the French began bombarding the forts at Yorktown, where Cornwallis had retreated with his men. Cornwallis found himself trapped between the French navy and the

American army. By October, his troops were dangerously low on food, arms, and supplies. On October 19, Cornwallis and his 8,000 soldiers (which equaled one-quarter of the British forces in America) had no choice but to surrender. A white flag was raised, causing all guns to fall silent. Then Cornwallis stepped toward the Continental army and offered his sword to George Washington.

While America was thrilled with this triumph, the British government was in shock. For the first time, Britain worried that it would actually lose the war and its American colonies. In the midst of heated commotion, Britain's Prime Minister Frederick North resigned. For England it was the beginning of the end of its colonial empire in North America.

The last major battle of the American War of Independence, the Battle of Yorktown, had gone on for six and a half years. Although some fighting between British and American soldiers continued, the British knew they were defeated. They had no choice but to negotiate a peace treaty and accept the fact that their former colonies were now an independent nation. The name of the resulting document was the Treaty of Paris.

4

The Treaty of Paris

On September 3, 1783, representatives of the British and American governments gathered together to sign the historic Treaty of Paris. David Hartley, a member of the British parliament, represented King George III. The son of a philosopher, Hartley was a politician and an inventor. He would become very close friends with Benjamin Franklin. Representing the new American nation were John Jay, John Adams, and Benjamin Franklin.

John Jay was a widely respected New York lawyer who represented New York at both Continental Congresses. Originally, Jay opposed independence from Britain (he wouldn't sign the Declaration of Independence). However, once the Revolution was under way, he was one of America's greatest supporters. From 1778 to 1789, he was president of the Continental Congress.

Jay arrived in Paris in 1782, to begin negotiating the peace treaty with the British along with another famous lawyer, John Adams. Adams, who was from Massachusetts, had been a revolutionary leader from the start. He was famous for having written many arguments against the

BENJAMIN FRANKLIN

In Paris, John Jay and John Adams were met by Benjamin Franklin. Franklin was an incredibly bright and talented man. Over the years, he had worked as a journalist, author, publisher, abolitionist, scientist, inventor, politician, and diplomat. A revolutionary leader, Franklin was renowned for his memorable speeches. He was a great speaker and was talented at making up memorable sayings. For example, he invented the popular phrase "A penny saved is a penny earned." He is also respected for his experiments with electricity. In his most famous experiment—to prove that lightning is a source of electricity—Franklin flew a kite in the middle of a rainstorm. During this extremely dangerous episode, he barely escaped electrocution. Aside from inventing the lightning rod, he invented the Franklin stove and bifocal glasses. He was responsible for founding America's first free public library (in Philadelphia in 1731). This act inspired other cities to open libraries of their own. In 1751, he helped establish the Pennsylvania Hospital, the first hospital in America. He also helped create America's first volunteer fire department. He organized the postal system as well. In 1775, as a result of his efforts, he became America's first postmaster general.

In the 1770s, Franklin was chosen to represent Pennsylvania in the Continental Congress. Here, he helped edit the Declaration of Independence. In 1776, he was sent to France as an American commissioner to try to persuade France to help America win the War of Independence. Franklin (who spoke perfect French) was such a success in Paris that many wealthy French families had portraits of him hanging in their salons. His close relationships with Louis XVI and members of the French government were largely responsible for France entering the war against Britain.

unjust British laws that were imposed on the colonies. Elected to the Massachusetts House of Representatives, he was also a member of the Continental Congress. A passionate speaker, he was very influential in convincing members of the Continental Congress to fight for independence from Britain. His talents resulted in his being chosen to help Jefferson write the Declaration of Independence.

Franklin played a major role in negotiating and writing America's Treaty of Paris with Britain. The treaty officially ended the Revolutionary War and recognized the United States of America as an independent nation. This had been the one item the American delegates had been charged by Congress to insist upon. In the end, they received a better settlement than the American Congress had ever thought possible. The final treaty contained ten parts, or articles.

Article 1 recognized the thirteen former British colonies as the United States of America.

Article 2 established the official boundaries between the United States and British North America (present-day Canada). The United States' territory stretched from the Great Lakes in the north to Florida in the south. Going inland from the Atlantic coast, all land extending west to the Mississippi River also belonged to the United States.

Article 3 dealt with an important economic issue. It granted fishing rights to American fishermen in the Grand Banks off the coast of Newfoundland and in the Gulf of Saint Lawrence. Both of these areas belonged to British North America.

Article 4 stated that prior to the war, all existing debts between America and Britain had to be honored. Essentially, this meant that money owed by the colonies to Britain had to be paid.

Article 5 declared that the United States Congress would "earnestly [strongly] recommend" to the governments of the thirteen states to recognize the rightful owners of all lands confiscated [seized] during the war. The states were to "provide for the restitution [return] of all estates [lands], rights and properties, which have been confiscated belonging to real British subjects." This restitution was never carried out.

Article 6, dealing with a similar issue, prevented the United States Congress from carrying out further confiscations of British land and properties. It also secured the rights of British citizens and Loyalists (colonists who had remained loyal to the British king) who chose to remain in the United States or who wished to return after having fled during the war.

Article 7 stated that prisoners of war on both sides were to be set free. All British soldiers were also to withdraw from American territory, which would put an end to all future hostilities. All property used by the British army in the United States was to be left in good condition (without being harmed or destroyed) and possessions or properties seized were to be returned, undamaged, to their rightful owners. (This notion of property extended to black slaves whom the army left behind.)

Article 8 gave both Great Britain and the United States equal and permanent access to the Mississippi River. The river was an essential trading and communications route that linked inland America to the sea and, subsequently, to the Atlantic coast, the Caribbean islands, the rest of the Americas, and Europe.

Article 9 ordered any territories captured between the end of the war and the approval of the Treaty of Paris to be returned to their rightful owners.

Article 10 stated that the Treaty of Paris had to be ratified (approved) by both the American and British governments. American and British representatives had six months following the signing of the document in Paris to accomplish this ratification.

This page outlining the specifics of Article 10 of the Treaty of Paris features the wax seals and signatures of (from left to right) David Hartley, John Adams, Benjamin Franklin, and John Jay.

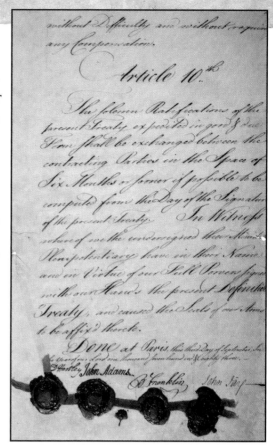

The requirements of this last article were never met. After the treaty was signed in Paris on September 3, 1783, it needed to be ratified by the British and American governments. By the time the document arrived from Europe to the United States, more than three months had passed. It was now mid-December. Congress was not in session and many delegates were on holiday. Of the thirteen states, representatives from only seven were present at Annapolis, Maryland.

A series of conflicts and discussions followed, which Thomas Jefferson describes in his autobiography. The problems stemmed from the fact that, according to American law (as it was spelled out in the Articles of Confederation), no treaty could be ratified without the majority approval of two-thirds (nine out of thirteen) of the states. Jefferson, who was present as a delegate to Virginia, suggested dispatching messengers by boat to the other colonies. He argued that representatives from absent states could quickly sign the treaty and have it returned as rapidly as possible. Jefferson's suggestion was ruled out as being too expensive. However, if Congress waited for delegates from absent states to make the trip to Annapolis, there was a serious risk that the approved treaty would arrive late in Paris. And if the Americans missed the six-month deadline, the treaty would not be valid.

⚊ Behind the Scenes with Jefferson ⚊

Thomas Jefferson was a careful observer and talented writer. In his autobiography, a section of which is reproduced below, he describes (with clear irritation) Congress's discussions of ratifying the Treaty of Paris:

Our body was little numerous, but very contentious [argumentative]. Day after day was wasted on the most unimportant questions. My colleague [John] Mercer was one of those afflicted with the morbid rage of debate, of an ardent [passionate] mind, prompt imagination, and copious [abundant] flow of words, he heard with impatience any logic which was not his own. Sitting near me on some occasion of a trifling [insignificant] but wordy debate, he asked how I could sit in silence hearing so much false reasoning which a word should refute [disagree]? I observed to him that to refute indeed was easy, but to silence impossible.

That this was a waste and abuse of the time and patience of the house which could not be justified. And I believe that if the members of deliberative bodies were to observe this course generally, they

N E W - Y O R K, November 26.

Laſt Sunday night arrived the Lord Hyde Packet, in 47 days from Falmouth. From the Engliſh papers brought we have extracted the following important ADVICES:

L O N D O N, September 30.

THE
Definitive Treaty,

Between GREAT-BRITAIN and the UNITED STATES of America, ſign-ed at Paris the 3d day of September, 1783.

In the Name of the moſt holy and undivided Trinity.

IT having pleaſed the Divine Providence to diſ-poſe the hearts of the moſt ſerene and moſt po-tent prince George the third, by the grace of God, king of Great-Britain, France and Ireland, defender of the faith, duke of Brunſwick and Lunenburgh, arch-treaſurer and prince elector of the holy Roman empire, &c. and of the United-States of America, to forget all paſt miſunder-ſtandings and differences that have unhappily in-terrupted the good correſpondence and friendſhip which they mutually wiſh to reſtore, and to eſtab-liſh ſuch a beneficial and ſatisfactory intercourſe between the two countries, upon the ground of reciprocal advantages and mutual convenience, as may promote and ſecure to both perpetual peace and harmony; and having for this deſir-able end already laid the foundation of peace and reconciliation, by the proviſional articles ſigned at Paris on the 30th of November, 1782, by the commiſſioners empowered on each part, which articles were agreed to be inſerted in, and to conſtitute the treaty of peace propoſed to be ...

the middle of the ſaid river into Lake Ontario; through the middle of the ſaid lake until it ſtrikes the communication by water between that lake and Lake Erie; thence along the middle of ſaid communication into Lake Erie, through the mid-dle of ſaid lake, until it arrives at the water communication between that lake and Lake Hu-ron, thence through the middle of ſaid lake to the water communication between that lake and Lake Superior; thence through Lake Superior, northward of the iſles Royal and Phelipeaux to the Long Lake; thence through the middle of ſaid Long Lake and the water communication between it and the Lake of the Woods, to the ſaid lake of the Woods, thence through the ſaid lake to the moſt north-weſtern point thereof, and from thence on a due weſt courſe to the river Miſſiſſippi; thence by a line to be drawn along the middle of the ſaid river Miſſiſſippi; thence by a line to be drawn along the middle of the ſaid river Miſſiſſippi until it ſhall interſect the northernmoſt part of the thirty firſt degree of north latitude. So ..., by a line to be drawn due eaſt from the determination of the line laſt mentioned in the latitude of thirty-one degrees north of the equator, to the middle of the river Apalachicola or Catahouche; thence along the ...

and that Congreſs ſhall alſo earneſtly recommend to the ſeveral ſtates a reconſideration and reviſion of all acts or laws regarding the premiſes, ſo as to render the ſaid laws or acts perfectly conſiſt-ent; not only with juſtice and equity, but with that ſpirit of conciliation, which, on the return of the bleſſings of peace, ſhould univerſally pre-vail: and that Congreſs ſhall alſo earneſtly re-commend to the ſeveral ſtates, that the eſtates, rights and properties of ſuch laſt mentioned per-ſons ſhall be reſtored to them, they refunding to any perſons who may be now in poſſeſſion the bona fide price (where any has been given) which ſuch perſons may have paid on purchaſing any of the ſaid lands, rights or properties ſince the con-fiſcation.

And it is agreed, that all perſons who have a-ny intereſt in confiſcated lands, either by debts, marriage ſettlements, or otherwiſe, ſhall meet with no lawful impediment in the proſecution of their juſt rights.

Art. 6. That there ſhall be no future confiſ-cations made, nor any proſecutions commenced againſt any perſon or perſons for, or by reaſon of the part which he or they may have taken in ...

The Treaty of Paris (shown above) was signed September 3, 1783. The last page of the treaty (not shown here, but for a transcription of Articles I and III, see page 56) bears the signatures of David Hartley, who represented Great Britain, and the three American negotiators, who signed their names in alphabetical order.

would do in a day what takes them a week, and it is really more questionable, than may at first be thought, whether [Napoléon] Bonaparte's dumb legislature which said nothing and did much, may not be preferable to one which talks much and does nothing. I served with General Washington in the leg-islature of Virginia before the revolution, and, during it, with Dr. [Benajmin] Franklin in Congress. I never heard either of them speak ten minutes at a time, nor to any but the main point which was to decide the question. They laid their shoulders to the great points, knowing that the little ones would follow of themselves.

Finally, the situation was resolved in mid-January, when delegates from Connecticut and South Carolina arrived in the capital and lent their voices to the seven other states. The Treaty of Paris was unanimously (with the agreement of all present) approved on January 14, 1784, and sent on to Paris. Although the official deadline was missed, the Treaty of Paris was finally ratified by Britain on April 17, 1784. Its terms were respected by the governments and citizens of both Great Britain and the United States of America.

5

A New Nation

The day the Treaty of Paris was finalized, the United States of America was officially considered by all nations to be an independent nation. However, once the soldiers had all returned home, it was time to decide what kind of government this new nation would have.

⌒ The Articles of Confederation ⌒

As soon as America decided to break free from British rule, the leaders of the Continental Congress began to act as America's central government. One of its first duties was to draw up a set of rules that would define the role of the new federal government. More specifically, it would outline its organization, duties, and obligations. These rules were known as the Articles of Confederation.

It was difficult to come up with a document that all delegates would agree upon. Many delegates feared that a central, or federal, government would have too much power. Their concerns resulted in five years of arguments and debates. Finally, all thirteen states approved the Articles of Confederation in March 1781.

⇌ The Constitution ⇌

Unfortunately, the document that was finally approved gave very little authority to the new federal government. Already used to having their own local governments, the thirteen states were unwilling to give up any power. Furthermore, years of being subject to unfair British rule made the states suspicious of a strong, central government.

Among other problems, the federal government they created had no president and no federal justice system. It had no authority to control trade between the states and no means of raising taxes (and therefore no money). There was no national army to enforce decisions. Instead, states preferred to depend on their own individual militias.

Because the government was weak, when arguments broke out between individual states, there was no way of resolving them. And it wasn't long before many disputes took place. Between 1781 and 1788, many rebellions and trade disputes broke out as debts between states went unpaid and tensions grew.

The members of the Continental Congress worried that these disagreements between the individual states would end up tearing apart the fragile union. To resolve these conflicts, two members of Congress, James Madison of Virginia and Alexander Hamilton of New York, invited delegates from all the states to a convention in Philadelphia. What became known as the Constitutional Convention began on May 25, 1787. A constitution is a country's written system of rules that outlines the powers and duties of the government and protects citizens' rights. Representatives from twelve states were present at the convention. There were no delegates from Rhode Island, which was satisfied with the Articles of Confederation.

The fifty-five men who did attend were subsequently known as America's Founding Fathers. These men—who were responsible for the creation of the United States—possessed an impressive variety of talents and experiences. Some were farmers and businessmen, others were doctors and lawyers. The majority had university educations. Many had fought in the Revolution, and most held jobs in the governments of their home states. In age, they ranged from twenty-six to eighty-one.

Throughout the summer of 1787, the Founding Fathers debated many forms of government under the supervision of George Washington. Everything discussed at the convention was top secret. Guards were hired to chase away spies and eavesdroppers. Delegates could not even write letters home to say what was going on. Some delegates became fed up and left. However, those who remained wrote the 4,400-word document that became the United States Constitution. Among the important contributors were Washington, Benjamin Franklin, James Madison, and Alexander Hamilton.

After the conflicts caused by the states' different interpretations of the Articles of Confederation, the Founding Fathers felt it was necessary to create a powerful federal government to maintain a strong, harmonious nation. This federal government was made up of three important branches: executive (the president), legislative (Congress), and judicial (the Supreme Court). These three branches (which were all of equal importance) constituted a system of checks and balances that prevented any one branch from having too much power and abusing citizens' rights. The Constitution stated that no branch could make decisions or pass laws without the approval of the other two branches.

Congress was made up of two houses. The House of Representatives united delegates from all the states. The number of representatives was based on each state's population. For example, at the time, Virginia (which had a large population) had more representatives than New Jersey. Meanwhile, in the Senate, each state had the same number of representatives, called senators. Congress was in charge of passing laws, raising taxes, regulating the national economy, and declaring war. The president's job was to carry out the laws passed by Congress, to make decisions about foreign affairs, and to command the military. The federal courts had the power to reject laws passed by Congress or state governments that they believed disagreed with the Constitution.

On September 17, 1787, the completed Constitution was signed by thirty-nine of the Founding Fathers. Thirteen had already gone home and another three refused to sign. Although the majority of delegates had approved it, the Constitution also had to be ratified by at least a majority of nine out of thirteen states. Founding Fathers James Madison, Alexander Hamilton, and John Jay wrote arguments in support of the Constitution. Published in the country's most widely read newspapers, these were known as the Federalist Papers because they argued for a strong central government. However, many states worried about having a Constitution that gave so much power to the federal government. Nonetheless, one by one, they came around. In June 1788, amid much celebrating, the approved Constitution became the supreme law of the land.

With the Constitution approved, America's first government could be formed. Members of Congress were chosen by each of the states to sit in the Senate and the House of Representatives. Meanwhile, George Washington was elected as the first president of the United States. After the War of Independence, Washington had wanted to return home to his family and farm in Mount Vernon, Virginia. However, he could hardly refuse the people's wishes. As leader of the Continental Congress and the commander in chief of the army, Washington had proven himself to be an intelligent, honest, loyal, and courageous man who knew a great deal about America and its people.

He was sworn in as president on April 30, 1789, in the nation's first capital, New York City. Crowds went wild with joy as he took the presidential oath. Washington chose two other Founding Fathers to hold important posts in his cabinet. As secretary of state, Thomas Jefferson was to deal with foreign policy. Meanwhile, as secretary of the treasury, Alexander Hamilton was in charge of the government's finances.

As the United States' first leaders, Washington and his government set to work creating many of the American systems and institutions that still exist today. First on their agenda was the creation of the justice system. The president was in charge of choosing the justices of the Supreme Court, the highest court in the land. The chief justice was John Jay,

Pictured above is a detail of the balcony of Federal Hall in New York City, where President George Washington was inaugurated on April 30, 1789. America's first president, Washington was a hero of the American Revolution and the Constitutional Convention.

who had signed the Treaty of Paris. Presided over by Jay, the Court met for the first time on February 2, 1789, to discuss what its specific duties would be. It took another two and a half years before the Supreme Court heard its first case.

Washington's government created federal taxes, banking, financial, and postal systems. Federal taxes raised money for the government to carry out its projects. American money was printed, and in New York, the stock exchange was opened. Washington also felt that it was very important to begin expanding westward. As a result, by the end of 1795, the United States territories extended all the way to the Mississippi River.

In 1790, the nation's capital moved from New York City to Philadelphia. This move was only temporary. In 1791, George Washington chose the swamplands around the

This print shows the fertile swampland of what was at the time known as George Town. This idyllic spot located by the Potomac River would eventually become the seat of the American government, Washington, D.C. It was felt that the location was a perfect midpoint for the northern and the southern states. Inhabitants have been referring to the city as Washington since 1791.

Potomac River as the site where a new capital would be constructed. It took ten years to build this shining new city. It was named Washington, D.C., in honor of America's favorite hero and first president. In 1800, Washington, D.C., replaced Philadelphia as the nation's capital. One of the key planners of the city was Thomas Jefferson.

⹀ The Bill of Rights ⹀

In order to get the state governments to approve the Constitution, the Founding Fathers had promised to make additions to it at a later date. These additions, known as amendments, would constitute the Bill of Rights. The purpose of the United States Bill of Rights was to address the states' worries about federal abuses of power by defending the rights of states and their citizens. Prior to the Revolution, many of the colonial governments had penned their own bills of rights that protected the individuals' basic liberties. Many were based on England's Bill of Rights, which had been written in 1689. During discussions about the Constitution, Thomas Jefferson, author of the Declaration of Independence and future third president, wrote a letter to his friend James Madison. In it, he said: "A bill of rights is what the people are entitled to against every government on earth."

It was Madison, in fact, who ended up drafting most of the Bill of Rights. He originally wrote seventeen amendments, which were later reduced to ten. Approved by Congress in 1789, and ratified by the majority of states in 1791, these ten amendments outlined the basic rights of all American citizens.

Among the rights guaranteed by this historic document were free speech; freedom of the press; freedom to practice all religions; freedom to meet in public; freedom against unreasonable searches and seizures in one's home; the right to bear arms; the right to a speedy, public trial by jury; the right to an attorney when accused of a crime; the right to reasonable bail; and the right to no cruel or unusual punishment.

The rights and liberties set down in the Bill of Rights are eternal and sacred. They can never be taken away by any government or court of justice. They have become the spirit and backbone of American society. To many, they define the best of what it is to be an American.

Timeline

≈ **1763** The end of the French and Indian War. Britain wins French territories in North America. In order to pay for the costs of war, the British king taxes American colonists.

≈ **1765** Britain passes the Stamp Act, which requires all newspapers and legal documents to carry a stamp purchased from Britain. American colonists are furious and succeed in getting the British government to repeal the tax.

≈ **1767** Britain passes the Townshend Acts, a series of new taxes on glass, paper, tea, paints, and other goods shipped to the colonies from Britain. The colonists protest and refuse to buy British goods.

≈ **1770** The Boston Massacre breaks out between colonists and British soldiers in Boston. Soldiers shoot townspeople, ultimately killing five. The Townshend Acts are repealed, leaving only the tax on tea.

≈ **1773** Britain passes the Tea Act. In response, colonists calling themselves the Sons of Liberty board British ships and dump forty-five tons of tea into Boston Harbor, an event later known as the Boston Tea Party.

≈ **1774** In response to the Boston Tea Party, Britain passes four laws known as the Intolerable Acts in order to punish the disobedient colonists. United against Britain, elected leaders from each colony attend the First Continental Congress in Philadelphia.

≈ **1775** The Battles of Lexington and Concord are the first major battles between American colonists and British forces in what will become the Revolutionary War. The Second Continental Congress is held in Philadelphia. Delegates from the thirteen colonies meet. They create their own Continental army and elect George Washington as its commander in chief.

≈ **1776** The Declaration of Independence is approved by the Continental Congress on July 4. Washington crosses the Delaware River.

≈ **1777** Winter at Valley Forge.

≈ **1778** France enters the war against the British after signing a treaty with America.

≈ **1779** Spain enters the war as an American ally.

≈ **1781** The British surrender to American forces at the Battle of Yorktown.

≈ **1781** The Articles of Confederation are adopted.

≈ **1783** The Treaty of Paris is signed on September 3, officially ending the Revolutionary War against Britain and recognizing the United States of America as an independent nation.

≈ **1784** The Treaty of Paris is ratified by the U.S. Congress on January 14, 1784.

≈ **1787** The Constitutional Convention approves the Constitution of the United States of America.

≈ **1789** George Washington is elected first president of the United States. The Bill of Rights is approved by Congress.

and in Virtue of our Full Powers
with our Hands the present Dep
Treaty, and caused the Seals of our

Primary Source Transcriptions

Page 12: Excerpt from the Stamp Act

Transcription

An act for granting and applying certain stamp duties, and other duties, in the British colonies and plantations in America, towards further defraying the expences of defending, protecting, and securing the same; and for amending such parts of the several acts of parliament relating to the trade and revenues of the said colonies and plantations, as direct the manner of determining and recovering the penalties and forfeitures therein mentioned.

WHEREAS by an act made in the last session of parliament, several duties were granted, continued, and appropriated, towards defraying the expences of defending, protecting, and securing, the British colonies and plantations in America: and whereas it is just and necessary, that provision be made for raising a further revenue within your Majesty's dominions in America, towards defraying the said expences: we, your Majesty's most dutiful and loyal subjects, the commons of Great Britain in parliament assembled, have therefore resolved to give and grant unto your Majesty the several rates and duties herein after mentioned; and do most humbly beseech your Majesty that it may be enacted, and be it enacted by the King's most excellent majesty, by and with the advice and consent of the lords spiritual and temporal, and commons, in this present parliament assembled, and by the authority of the same, That from and after the first day of November, one thousand seven hundred and sixty five, there shall be raised, levied, collected, and paid unto his Majesty, his heirs, and successors, throughout the colonies and plantations in America which now are, or hereafter may be, under the dominion of his Majesty, his heirs and successors . . .

Page 22: Excerpt from the Declaration of Independence

Transcription

When, in the course of human events, it becomes necessary for one people to dissolve the political bonds which have connected them with another, and to assume among the powers of the earth, the separate and equal station to which the laws of nature and of nature's God entitle them, a decent respect to the opinions of mankind requires that they should declare the causes which impel them to the separation.

We hold these truths to be self-evident, that all men are created equal, that they are endowed by their Creator with certain unalienable rights, that among these are life, liberty and the pursuit of happiness. That to secure these rights, governments are instituted among men, deriving their just powers from the consent of the governed. That whenever any form of government becomes destructive to these ends, it is the right of the people to alter or to abolish it, and to institute new government, laying its foundation on such principles and organizing its powers in such form, as to them shall seem most likely to effect their safety and happiness. Prudence, indeed, will dictate that governments long established should not be changed for light and transient causes; and accordingly all experience hath shown that mankind are more disposed to suffer, while evils are sufferable, than to right themselves by abolishing the forms to which they are accustomed. But when a long train of abuses and usurpations, pursuing invariably the same object evinces a design to reduce them under absolute despotism, it is their right, it is their duty, to throw off such government, and to provide new guards for their future security. —Such has been the patient sufferance of these colonies; and such is now the necessity which constrains them to alter their former systems of government. The history of the present King of Great Britain is a history of repeated injuries and usurpations, all having in direct object the establishment of an absolute tyranny over these states. To prove this, let facts be submitted to a candid world.

Page 42: Articles 1 and 3 from the Treaty of Paris

Transcription

Article I. There shall be a Christian, universal, and perpetual peace, as well by sea as by land, and a sincere and constant friendship shall be re established between their Britannick, Most Christian, Catholick, and Most Faithful Majesties, and between their heirs and successors, kingdoms, dominions, provinces, countries, subjects, and vassals, of what quality or condition soever they be, without exception of places or of persons: So that the high contracting parties shall give the greatest attention to maintain between themselves and their said dominions and subjects this reciprocal friendship and correspondence, without permitting, on either side, any kind of hostilities, by sea or by land, to be committed from henceforth, for any cause, or under any pretence whatsoever, and every thing shall be carefully avoided which might hereafter prejudice the union happily re-established, applying themselves, on the contrary, on every occasion, to procure for each other whatever may contribute to their mutual glory, interests, and advantages, without giving any assistance or protection, directly or indirectly, to those who would cause any prejudice to either of the high contracting parties: there shall be a general oblivion of every thing that may have been done or committed before or since the commencement of the war which is just ended.

III. All the prisoners made, on all sides, as well by land as by sea, and the hostages carried away or given during the war, and to this day, shall be restored, without ransom, six weeks, at least, to be computed from the day of the exchange of the ratification of the present treaty, each crown respectively paying the advances which shall have been made for the subsistance and maintenance of their prisoners by the Sovereign of the country where they shall have been detained, according to the attested receipts and estimates and other authentic vouchers which shall be furnished on one side and the other. And securities shall be reciprocally given for the payment of the debts which the prisoners shall have contracted in the countries where they have been detained until their entire liberty. And all the ships of war and merchant vessels Which shall have been taken since the expiration of the terms agreed upon for the cessation of hostilities by sea shall likewise be restored, bon fide, with all their crews and cargoes: and the execution of this article shall be proceeded upon immediately after the exchange of the ratifications of this treaty.

*and in Virtue of our Full Power
with our Hands the present Def
Treaty, and caused the Seals of our*

Glossary

abolitionist A person who works to outlaw slavery.

amendment An addition to the U.S. Constitution.

ammunition Explosive military material such as bullets or bombs.

banned To be outlawed; prohibited.

bifocal A lens for eyeglasses that corrects both nearsightedness and farsightedness.

boycott To refuse to deal with a person or business as a form of protest.

constitution A country's written system of rules that outlines the powers and duties of the government and protects citizens' rights.

Continental Congress The political body that functioned as America's first government and directed the War of Independence.

currency Money.

Declaration of Independence An official document approved on July 4, 1776, in which American colonists declared themselves free from British rule.

delegate A representative elected to attend a political gathering.

intolerable Unbearable.

militia An army of private citizens that is called upon to fight in times of emergency.

persecuted Discriminated against.

ratify To approve a law, document, or action.

repeal To do away with or cancel, especially a law or act.

retaliate To fight or strike back.

secretary of state A person in a government who is in charge of that country's relationships with other countries.

surrender To give up completely; to admit loss to one's enemy.

tolerant Sympathetic to or accepting of a wide range of different beliefs or practices.

tyranny Oppressive, authoritarian power exerted by a government over its people.

For More Information

WEB SITES

Due to the changing nature of Internet links, the Rosen Publishing Group, Inc., has developed an online list of Web sites related to the subject of this book. This site is updated regularly. Please use this link to access the list:

http://www.rosenlinks.com/psat/trpa

For Further Reading

Allen, Thomas B. *George Washington, Spymaster: How the Americans Outspied the British and Won the Revolutionary War*. Washington, D.C.: National Geographic Books, 2004.

George, Lynn. *A Time Line of the American Revolution*. New York, NY: Rosen Publishing Group, Inc., 2003.

Giblin, James, and Michael Dooling. *The Amazing Life of Benjamin Franklin*. New York, NY: Scholastic, 2001.

Murray, Stuart. *Eyewitness: American Revolution*. New York, NY: DK Publishing, 2002.

Wood, Gordon S. *The American Revolution: A History*. New York, NY: Modern Library, 2002.

Bibliography

George, Lynn. *A Time Line of the American Revolution*. New York, NY: Rosen Publishing Group, Inc., 2003.

Jefferson, Thomas. *Autobiography 1743–1790*. The Avalon Project at Yale Law School. Retrieved October 12, 2004 (http://www.yale.edu/lawweb/avalon/jeffauto.htm#treatydebate).

Kidport Reference Library. "The American Revolution." Retrieved September 14, 2004 (http://www.kidport.com/RefLib/UsaHistory/AmericanRevolution/AmerRevolution.htm).

"Liberty! The American Revolution." PBS Online companion to the television series. Retrieved November 3, 2004 (http:// www.pbs.org/ktca/liberty/index.html).

Primary Source Image List

Cover: 1783 oil-on-canvas painting entitled *The Signing of the Treaty of Paris* by Benjamin West. Housed in the U.S. Senate in Washington, D.C.

Page 5: Hand-colored lithographic map of French and British dominions in North America. Published by W. Richardson between 1755 and 1789. Printed for I. Covens and C. Mortier in the Netherlands.

Page 8: An etching from 1782, called *The Belligerent Plenipo*, published in 1782, and created by Dutch artist Thomas Colley.

Page 11: A mid–nineteenth-century engraving of portrait, *The Death of General Wolfe*, by Benjamin West. Created in Boston, Massachusetts.

Page 12: *Proof Sheet of 1d Stamp Duties for Newspapers* dating from 1765. Board of Inland Revenues Stamping Department Archive, Philatelic Collection, the British Library, London, England.

Page 14: A newspaper page (woodcut and letterpress) from March 12, 1770, showing the coffins of four men killed in the Boston Massacre. From *The Boston Gazette and Country Journal*.

Page 16: Engraving of George Robert Twelves Hewes, published in the *Boston Tea Party* magazine, in June 1893. By unknown artist.

Page 18: 1789 engraving called *Boston Tea Party* by W. D. Cooper. Housed at the Library of Congress.

Page 21: Title page from first edition of Thomas Paine's *Common Sense*. Printed in 1776, by R. Bell in Philadelphia, Pennsylvania.

Page 22: The *Dunlap Broadside*, printed by John Dunlap on July 8, 1776. The text was written by Thomas Jefferson and approved by U.S. Congress.

Page 26: Watercolor on paper of an American soldier. Nineteenth-century copy of 1777 original by Friedrich Konstantin von Germann. Housed at the New York Public Library.

Page 29: Eastman Johnson's copy of Emmanuel Leutze's painting *Washing Crossing the Delaware*. From a private collection. Leutze's original is housed in the Metropolitan Museum of New York.

Page 33: John Trumbull's 1787 oil-on-canvas painting *The Surrender of Cornwallis at Yorktown*. Commissioned in 1817; purchased in 1820. Housed in the U.S. Capitol.

Page 36: Joseph Siffred Duplessis' portrait of Benjamin Franklin, housed at the Petit Palais in Paris, France.

Page 42: The Treaty of Paris, published in Philadelphia, Pennsylvania, and printed by David C. Claypoole in 1783.

Page 49: Photo of a copper engraving of the inauguration of George Washington by Amos Doolittle, dated 1790.

Page 50: Copper engraving entitled *The City of Washington*, 1790. Created by T. Cartwright and printed by George Beck of Atkins & Nightengale in 1801.

Index

ABOUT THE AUTHOR

Lee Jedson grew up in Texas and attended the University of Texas at Austin, where he received a combined degree in history and literature. An American history buff, he has written several books for both children and adults. Aside from writing and reading, he dreams of running a small cattle ranch in rural Texas.

PHOTO CREDITS

Cover courtesy of the Diplomatic Reception Rooms, U.S. Dept. of State, Washington, D.C.; p. 5 Library of Congress, Geography and Map Division; pp. 8, 14, 21, 49 Library of Congress, Prints and Photograph Division; p. 11 Phillips Fine Art Auctioneers/Bridgeman Art Library; p. 12 the British Library; pp. 18, 42 Library of Congress, Rare Books and Manuscripts Division; pp. 22, 40 National Archives and Records Administration; p. 24 © Francis G. Mayer/Corbis; p. 26 Print Collection, Miriam and Ira D. Wallach Division of Art, Prints, and Photographs, the New York Public Library, Astor, Lenox, and Tilden Foundations; p. 29 Art Resource, NY; p. 33 photograph © 1986, the Detroit Institute of Arts; p. 36 Giraudon/Art Resource, NY; p. 50 I. N. Phelps Stokes Collection, Miriam and Ira D. Wallach Division of Art, Prints, and Photographs, the New York Public Library, Astor, Lenox and Tilden Foundations.

Designer: Evelyn Horovicz; Editor: Annie Sommers
Photo Researcher: Jeffrey Wendt